Piano / Vocal / Guitar

LA LA LAND

MUSIC FROM THE MOTION PICTURE SOUNDTRACK

ISBN 978-1-4950-8824-7

7777 W. BLUEMOUND RD. P.O. BOX 13819 MILWAUKEE, WI 53213

In Australia Contact:
Hal Leonard Australia Pty. Ltd.
4 Lentara Court
Cheltenham, Victoria, 3192 Australia
Email: ausadmin@halleonard.com.au

Visit Hal Leonard Online at
www.halleonard.com

ANOTHER DAY OF SUN

Music by JUSTIN HURWITZ
Lyrics by BENJ PASEK
& JUSTIN PAUL

3

when they let you down,   the

MIA & SEBASTIAN'S THEME

Music by
JUSTIN HURWITZ

SOMEONE IN THE CROWD

Music by JUSTIN HURWITZ
Lyrics by BENJ PASEK
& JUSTIN PAUL

Bright Broadway two-beat feel

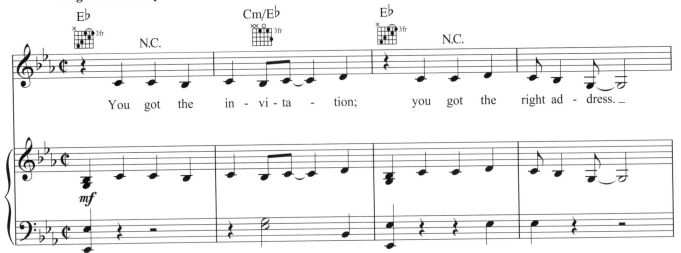

You got the in-vi-ta - tion; you got the right ad-dress. _

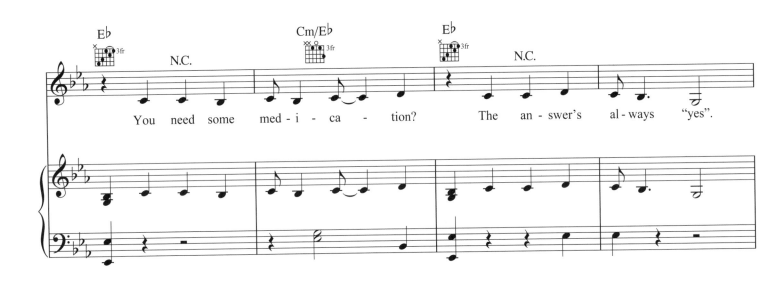

You need some med-i-ca - tion? The an-swer's al-ways "yes".

A lit-tle chance en-coun - ter could be the one you've wait -

stay be - hind. (You've got to go and ___ find...) ___

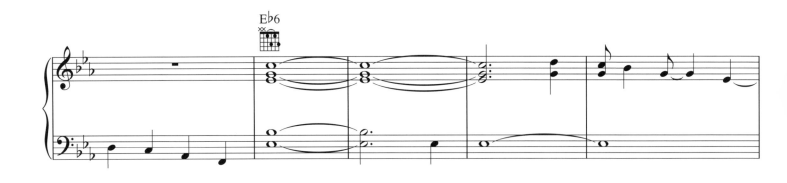

(Spoken): that some - one in ___ the crowd. ___

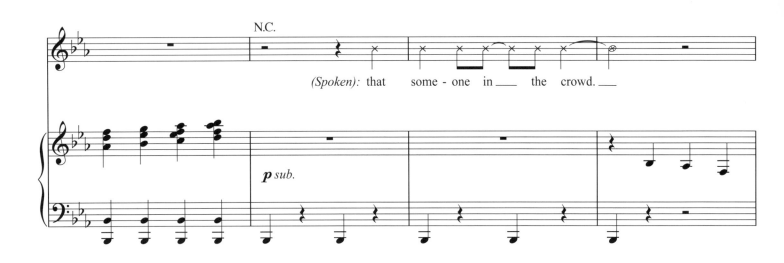

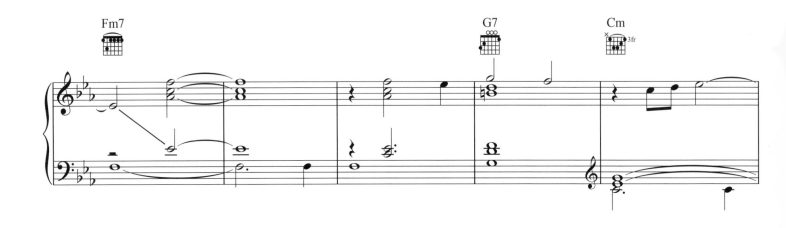

A LOVELY NIGHT

Music by JUSTIN HURWITZ
Lyrics by BENJ PASEK
& JUSTIN PAUL

Faster, straight eighths

CITY OF STARS

Music by JUSTIN HURWITZ
Lyrics by BENJ PASEK
& JUSTIN PAUL

PLANETARIUM

Music by
JUSTIN HURWITZ

Moderately fast

44

START A FIRE

Music & Lyrics by JOHN STEPHENS,
ANGÉLIQUE CINÉLU, MARIUS de VRIES
and JUSTIN HURWITZ

Slowly and freely

I don't know _

why I keep _ mov - in' _ my bod - y; _ I don't know _

if this _ is wrong _ or if it's right. _ I don't know _

* Recorded a half step higher.

don't you know __ I feel __ so good, I just know __ I feel __ so good _____

to - night. __

I don't care __ if this turns _ in - to a ri-

-ot; __ let's get reck - less, tear __ this place __ down to the floor. __

(We can start _ a fi-
Solo ends

D.S. al Coda

CODA

don't you know, _ don't you know, _____ to-night. _

EPILOGUE

Music by
JUSTIN HURWITZ

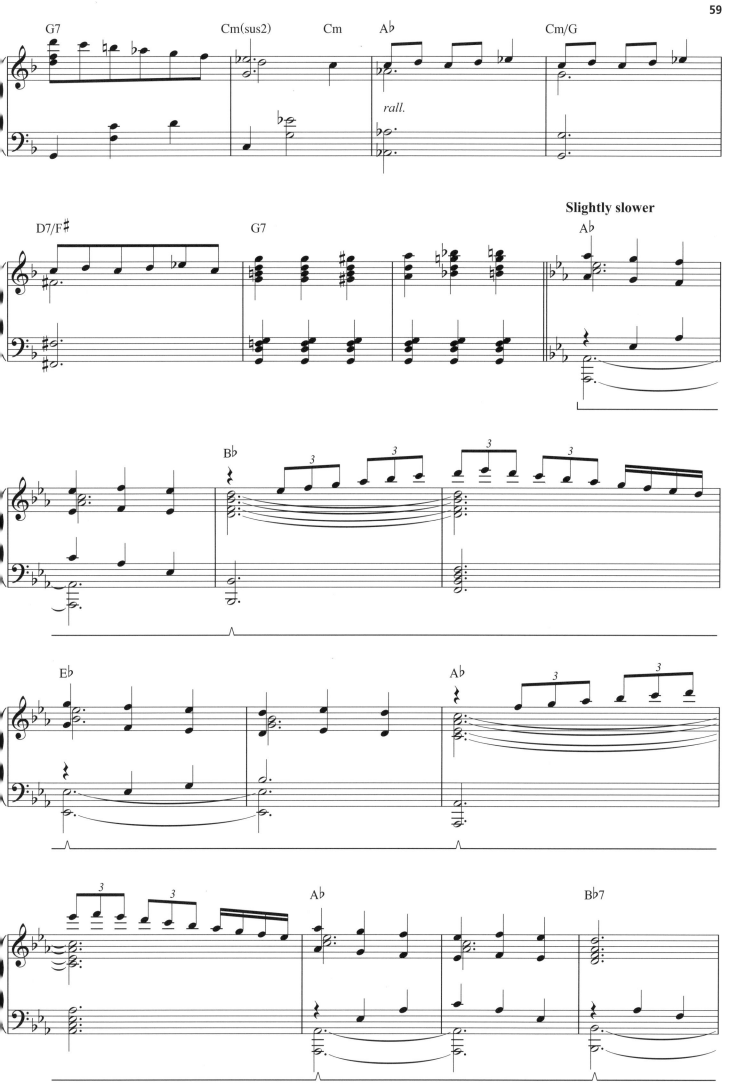

ENGAGEMENT PARTY

Music by
JUSTIN HURWITZ

Moderately, expressively

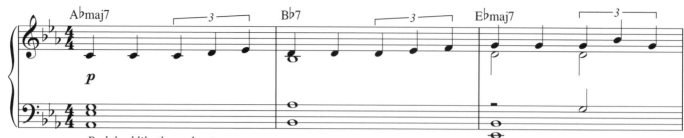

Pedal ad lib. throughout

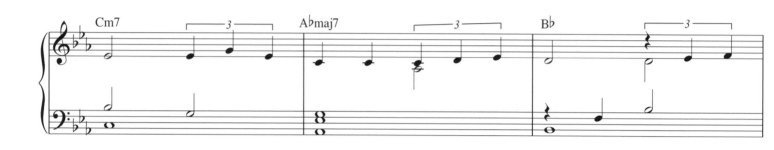

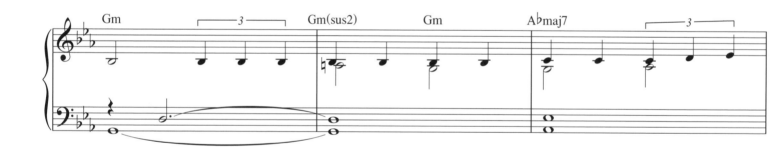

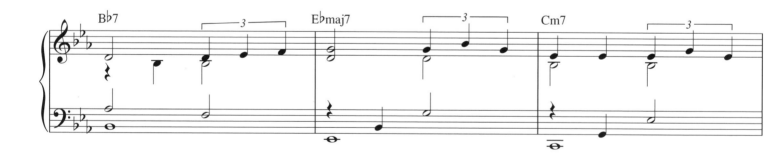

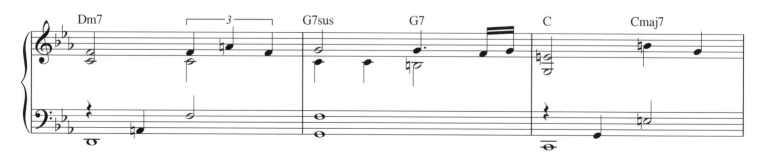

AUDITION
(The Fools Who Dream)

Music by JUSTIN HURWITZ
Lyrics by BENJ PASEK
& JUSTIN PAUL

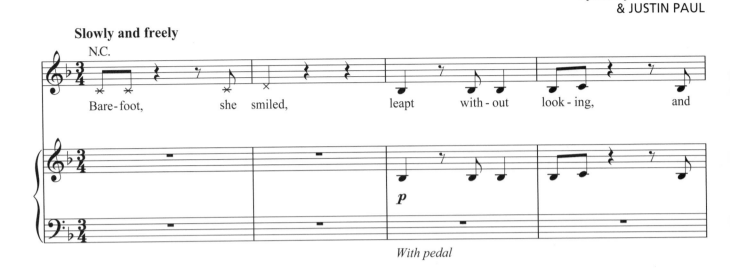

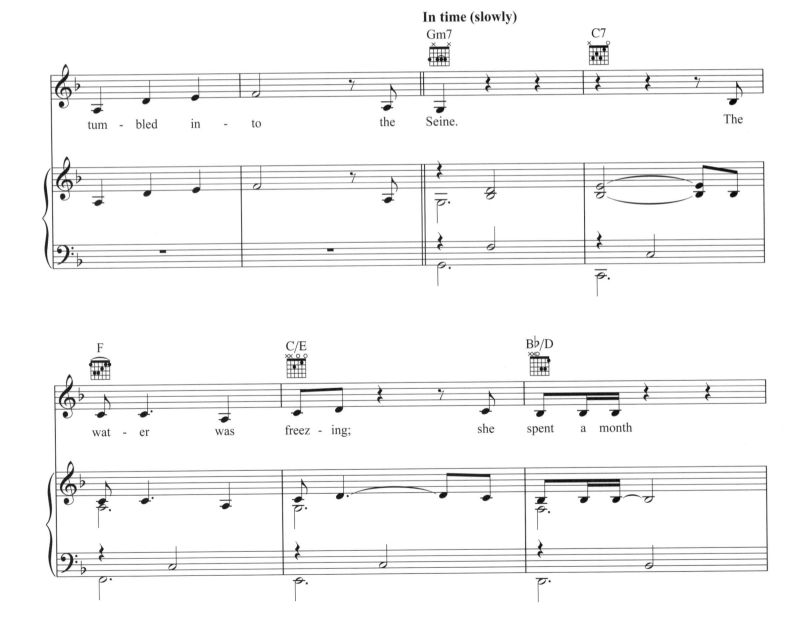